G000165984

The Secrets to Motivating Your Team

Joy Ogeh-Hutfield

ISBN: 978-0-9932299-9-2

Published in the United Kingdom in 2015
by Cambria Books, Wales, United Kingdom.

DEDICATION

Dedicated to those who are aspiring to achieve greatness in their own lives and in the way they impact others.

Most of all to Mark, Lauren, Isabelle, Daniel and Nadia.

CONTENTS

INTRODUCTION

Motivation is the key to a happy and productive workforce.

As people, we are complex and inconsistent. We react to the same event differently depending on our interpretation of the situation or how we are feeling at that particular time. So, working in or with a team comes a clash of cultures, egos and personalities. Motivation is intrinsic. It therefore varies from individual to individual, and what motivates one person may not motivate the other.

Teams have the power to increase both productivity and morale as well as destroy them. When teams work effectively, they can make better decisions, solve more complex challenges and are more creative, sometimes going the extra mile. To be successful today in any walk of life requires the use of collective knowledge and the richness of diverse perspectives.

PART ONE

What Can *Demotivate* a Team?

WHAT CAN DEMOTIVATE A TEAM?

My first experience of working in a professional team set up was as a lecturer, fresh from university. This was to be the catalyst in giving me an insight into managing and working effectively as a team member. It was to become a valuable lesson as a director and also as a businesswoman.

As a lecturer, I was part of a team that worked with adults with learning difficulties and disabilities. I was assigned a classroom assistant who had been at the college for some time and had harnessed a very negative attitude. Every idea I had about innovative ways of working with the students was greeted with - "No that won't work here" or "the students can't do that". After weeks of dealing with her negativity I had had enough. Her impact on me was one of frustration plus I felt undermined all the time.

It all came to a head at a staff meeting while we were planning for the following term. As I stood up and began to share my ideas on how we could move forward with some of the initiatives, she started to interrupt in her usual style of – "we have tried that before and it didn't work". At that point, all my pent up frustration came to the boil and I found myself shouting at her.

Of course, the other lecturers looked at me in shock horror. She was made to look like the good person, while I came across as aggressive and insulting. This did not go down well as I came out of the meeting feeling very demotivated and for weeks I did not have the confidence to contribute to any team meetings.

After ~~the incident we did come together~~ to resolve our differences and developed a healthier working relationship.

Working as part of a team can be very rewarding as well as frustrating. It can bring out the best in us or the worst. The fact is that no one quite prepares us for the world of work or working as a part of a team. Individuals are expected to just get on with it. They either swim or sink.

However, on reflection of the incident, I came out with some key learning points. Her negativity, and lack of respect and appreciation of the values and qualities I brought as a team member coupled with my own lack of communication skills and not sharing how I felt about her attitude and perhaps not also taking the time to understand her perspective meant that we could not give our best to the students we were meant to be serving.

So what happened here?

Here was a young girl, fresh from university, motivated, passionate, full of great ideas and energy, and ready to unleash her full potential. On the other hand was a person who had lost their drive, creativity and passion, and who was not open to innovative ways of thinking or doing things; and as a result had become very negative. This negativity, constant criticism, dismissal of ideas, the focus on mistakes instead of what had been done right and the frustration further undermined confidence and brought about demotivation. Sounds familiar?

So, what's the point?

Nobody comes into a business demotivated in the beginning. A negative environment brings frustration and demotivation. It kills the passion and the creativity.

If people are brought into a business environment, highly motivated and end up demotivated, it means that the mind-set within that particular environment is responsible for bringing about that demotivation. As long as the mind-set of the individuals within the environment remains the same, no matter how many motivated people are brought in, the result is likely to remain the same.

Change the environment by changing the mind-set of those who function in it, and they will feel empowered and ready to unleash their potential, and anyone who subsequently joins the business can be infected with that same positive mind-set and they too will be compelled to add greater value. Businesses are therefore losing out because of ineffective staff members or teams.

What Is The Cost Of An *Ineffective* Team?

WHAT IS THE COST OF AN INEFFECTIVE TEAM?

So, what is the cost to a business of one ineffective staff member or, even worse, a team?

I will tell you - billions in lost productivity and unresolved conflicts.

Let's take an example:

A manager and his two employees take three hours to resolve a conflict. The conflict costs £120 of his time, plus another £90 for his employees. If the manager has two conflicts a week for 52 weeks, this costs £21,840 a year and a loss of 312 hours.

Individuals create teams. If the individual is not harnessing the right mind-set, the team will be unable to function cooperatively or share ideas and be productive.

Before I share with you the secrets of motivating your staff/teams, let us find out what in the first place has demotivated them? I call these motivation killers or money drainers.

It is more likely that an individual who feels that there is a lack of respect for their work, intelligence or contribution will be demotivated. Also, if they feel they are not listened to, their opinions do not count or they are treated unfairly.

More importantly, things can escalate and take a downward spiral if they are not given the resources or creative freedom to work their magic. Demotivation is contagious!

Why Do Teams *Fail*?

WHY DO TEAMS FAIL?

These are some of the reasons why teams fail:

- Teams fail when there is a lack of understanding and a lack of communicating the vision.

- They can also fail when they do not understand and take the time to clarify their roles, purpose and goals. I call it 'The BIG WHY?' as in why do they do what they do?

- Another reason is the lack of focus on creativity and excellence.

- When individuals lack the mutual respect for each other, this can also bring about a break down in the team.

- A lack of respect and understanding for cultural differences, we all come from diverse and varying backgrounds. These cultural differences need to be taken into account. And when people do not see and acknowledge those cultural differences, teams can become ineffective.

- Working in a non-supportive and negative environment is also a key factor.

- Finally, the lack of skills updates, training

or progress.

Now that we have identified some of the reasons why teams fail, let us look at the cost of a demotivated team.

- One of the consequences of harnessing a demotivated team is low staff morale.

- Secondly, a lack of energy and passion for business objectives. Basically, people are just coming to work and are not sure where they fit in.

- High sickness rate and absenteeism: people do not want to be there, and so they are off sick.

- Billions in lost productivity and unresolved conflicts: when a team is demotivated, people are not in the right mind-set to produce outstanding results.

- Loss of great talent: your best people leave and so you are unlikely to recruit people who add value to your business.

- Finally, high staff turnover and recruitment costs: employees are leaving and you are spending more and more money recruiting people, and no sooner have they come in, they are out again.

So, we understand that having a demotivated team does have grave consequences.

Now that we are aware of some of the things that can demotivate your staff or teams, raising your awareness is the first key step to getting a solution.

I am going to share with you the secrets to motivating your teams.

The question is: *Can every staff member become a high performing staff member and can every team become a high performing team?*

Can Every Team Become a *High Performing* **Team?**

CAN EVERY TEAM BECOME A HIGH PERFORMING TEAM?

To motivate is to cause a shift in the way someone thinks, getting them to do or perform a task. The result can be instant. But it can easily wear out. Therefore, to transform is to sustain the processes. It is a deeper level of operating a radical shift that takes the individual or team to the next level. This is the level that produces outstanding results.

Once you have motivated your team, the key is to sustain and keep the fire going. As a transformation coach, I bring the two into alignment. When a mind-set is transformed there is a renewed way of thinking. Limiting beliefs are replaced by more empowering ones that causes them to perform and deliver with confidence.

Recruiting talent can be a costly and time consuming exercise. If you want to retain people, recognise that you will need to invest in them if you want to see a return on their talent. For example, if your sales teams are already doing a great job bringing in the sales and hitting all their targets, this is the right time to invest even more into developing their skills, which will get them to operate on a much higher level, challenging them to produce even greater results. As a business, you are more likely to see a quicker return on your investment. The general rule of thumb for most businesses is that they wait for the teams to start performing badly before they can even think of investing in them. The problem is, while they are contemplating whether it is worth their investment in terms of money, their business is losing thousands by the day due to unproductive teams. Therefore making an investment not only prevents problems occurring in the future, it sustains the momentum and reliability of the team.

On the other hand, imagine if every single one of your staff or team were motivated, productive, hitting all their targets, achieving soaring sales, outrageously creative, taking ownership and sharing ideas, and filled with a renewed sense of vision and purpose. Sounds like a dream right?

What would it take and what has to happen to make this your reality?

Think of a time you particularly felt motivated at work. What caused the change? What was the impact on yourself, on your work and on your colleagues?

While you are pondering on those questions, here are a few practical tools and strategies to unlock the potential of your team; the secrets to motivating your team.

PART TWO

The Secrets to **Motivating** *Your Team*

Become a
Motivating *Leader*

BECOME A MOTIVATING LEADER

When you are able to connect to yourself and others, you can begin your journey to creating a motivated workforce. Empowerment requires a major shift in attitude. It is the ability to bring out the power that resides in people's knowledge, experience and internal motivation.

The solution to any challenge is to raise your own awareness. Asking the right questions will provide you with the right solutions.

Here are a few questions to start you off:

Why do I want to motivate my team?

Have I got a clear vision of what I want to achieve?

How well and how often do I communicate the vision?

Does my team understand my expectations?

Do I give feedback in a timely and specific way?

Do I involve my team in decisions, especially those that affect them?

Is my attitude and personality empowering and motivating?

Am I open and trustworthy?

Have I created an open, trusting and fun environment?

Do I listen to my team on a regular basis?

How often do I personally thank and appreciate my team?

By asking these questions you can gain insight and clarity in how to begin the motivation process.

These questions also challenge you to take a closer look at your leadership and management style or input.

My motto:

To transform and motivate your team, you have to first transform and motivate yourself.

'No one is ever empowered by a miserable looking person or manager.'

First become the solution and the others will follow suit.

Most of us have heard the song 'Follow the Leader', as great as the concept sounds, if the leader is not motivated, the team will not be motivated either and reach its full potential. In most cases, teams mirror the behavior and attitude of their leader.

As a team leader, here are five choices you need to make to get you on your way to being the boss you should be.

ONE

Choose to be real – People buy into your vision. By being fake, you are in constant fear of being found out or caught out. You will lose credibility. One of the best and desirable qualities of a leader is to have an element of vulnerability about them. It is very attractive. It suggests that you are human and not a 'know all'. People will want to work with you to make things happen. Being real gives room for the acceptance of others.

TWO

Choose to lead from the position of appreciation – Master the art of appreciation. It keeps the fire in people's heart burning even in austere times, they will be willing to go the extra mile.

The principle of appreciation is about sowing a seed of value in someone. Sow now, reap tomorrow. It says 'you are important'. It brings out the very best in the individual, awakening their potential and allows the flow of creativity.

Harnessing this principle opens doors for a creative and dynamic workforce. An environment that does not operate on this principle can give way to a stressful and even oppressive atmosphere. Lead by example!

THREE

Choose to be a blessing to others – Refrain from speaking negatively about other people including those that work with and for you. Learn to always correct from the position of love and not of judgement. Making a negative judgement on a person creates distance and in time dims the light inside of them. You will make them too afraid to even try.

FOUR

Choose to believe in yourself and others - With this principle, a confident you is more likely to communicate a clearer vision. When you believe in others, you unlock their full potential. Do you remember that teacher or significant person in your life that believed in you against all odds? Belief allows people to do the impossible. Belief in yourself also allows you to operate on a higher dimension. You will dare to dream and see the world as your stage. A world of opportunities, not just for yourself, but for you to make a difference. 'The true goal of leadership is not to cross the finishing line first, but to take as many others with you.'

FIVE

Choose to LOVE - Yes, you heard me, it's not a spelling error!

Love is not a word often found in the business arena.

However, it's the most fundamental in the hierarchy of human needs. I am yet to come across a person who doesn't want to be loved.

Love frees us from making judgements. It allows us to see beyond the obvious. It makes room for transformational change.

Choosing to love the team that has been entrusted in your care is the greatest form of empowerment, trust and commitment. This is your 'Master Key' to motivating your team.

Now that you have understood what it takes to become a motivating leader, let's now unveil the secrets to how you can motivate your team.

SECRET NO.1

A Clear and Exciting
Vision of Success

A CLEAR AND EXCITING VISION OF SUCCESS

It is a must that every individual in the business buys into the vision, as that helps to create a corporate identity. Organisations, such as Samsung, Google and Apple, are reaping the benefits and the rewards of teams who have fully bought into their vision. Individual visions are therefore in complete alignment to the business vision and objectives.

One of the secrets, as you look to create an exciting vision for your teams, is to discuss the benefits of success. It is important that your teams understand what success can bring to them.

Take time to help them to explore the following questions:

- What role do they really play within the business?

- How well do they understand it?

- What is the BIG WHY for them?

- Do they understand why they do what they do?

These are some of the ways in which you can get your teams to begin to buy into your vision. If they understand it, it means they are able to sell the vision and operate in complete harmony to your business objectives.

Here is a quick exercise that you can do with your teams:

Organise a team meeting and get them to answer the questions posed earlier. I would advise you get someone external, not part of the team, to help debrief the session. Ask everyone to spend the next 30 minutes (allow more time if necessary) to write their individual vision of success in relevance to their role within the business. This is a very powerful and insightful exercise.

Work needs to provide individuals with a sense of fulfilment, they must know that they are adding value and doing something worthwhile. In other words - "Work must give a meaning".

SECRET NO.2

The Magic *of* **Rapport**

THE MAGIC OF RAPPORT

Another secret to motivating your teams can be found in the "Magic of Rapport". In creating this, it is about you getting to know the people in your teams. It is amazing how people feel motivated and assured when we take time to get to know them.

However, be mindful to create a healthy and respectable distance. Being BFFs with your team members is not always the best way to motivate them.

This is often a delicate balance to achieve. It is important to make your team members feel comfortable and see you as approachable, which opens the lines for communication. However, you don't want them to feel too comfortable, where they think it's 'ok' to turn up late and give excuses as to why they haven't delivered.

Here is a great exercise that I want you to do with your teams. It is awesome and goes a long way towards building rapport.

Get a whiteboard and write all the names of your team members. Get every team member to secretly write something they have accomplished and are proud of.

Take out 30 minutes from the working day and get the team members to match the accomplishments to the individuals in the team.

Once each member is successfully matched, the other team members must cheer and be genuinely happy for them.

Again, this is a fun way to build rapport and to recognise the talent pool that you have in your team.

SECRET NO.3

Appreciation *and* Recognition

APPRECIATION AND RECOGNITION

A great secret to motivating your team lies in "Appreciation and Recognition".

This is about creating a culture where these are encouraged, recognising their hard work and achievements. I will tell you, in all my years of working with teams, I have never heard an employee or team member complain about being appreciated too much! It works.

Check in individually with all of the members of the team – Recognise their strengths and work with them to put an action plan together to help them with their areas of improvement. While doing this, avoid using words like 'weakness' – they are disempowering. It is crucial that you get to know each one of them.

Ask them how they would like to be recognised, and acknowledge the different personalities within the team. For example, some might want a birthday card, or a hug, or a 'well done' card – whichever way, it's about making them feel important, wanted and needed.

When you appreciate people and recognise them for what they do, WOW, they are energised.

Here are some examples of practical exercises that I believe you can do very easily.

Designate a public whiteboard as a wall of recognition, where team members can jot down their colleagues' accomplishments for the rest to see.

Now, basic psychology indicates employees who are affirmed for good behaviour are more likely to repeat those actions and in the long run build a stronger business.

Secondly, get the team members to communicate their expectations of each other.

Get them to sit in a circle. A circle symbolises oneness, unity and wholeness.

Ask the individuals to communicate to their team members how they would like to be appreciated.

I recently conducted this exercise with a team during their team development day and the impact was powerful. The atmosphere was electrifying as the team members felt listened to and were able to express themselves. More importantly, they were treated with respect as individuals.

It is easy to feel undervalued and isolated as a single employee, separated from the big picture. This simple exercise will help them to understand the valuable role they are playing and how they are contributing to the success of the business.

SECRET NO.4

Developing Confidence *and* Belief

DEVELOPING CONFIDENCE AND BELIEF

Developing confidence and belief is my "Favourite Secret" to motivating your team.

When confidence is high and people believe in what they do, this will enable them to make better decisions and choices that will transform the team and its potential for achieving outstanding results. Confidence combats negativity and helps team members to share ideas openly and function cooperatively.

Let me share a story with you.

I recently worked with a sales team that was underperforming.

The picture was that morale was low, and the director was having a difficult time trying to motivate the team and get them to produce the results they needed to achieve their annual targets.

Now, one of the team members had been performing so badly, that they were considering letting her go. During the team transformation programme I provided, I was able to work with the individuals, using the inside-out approach, where we work firstly on their inner states and internal conflicts. One of the things that struck me was the fact that the majority of the team were so low in confidence, and now lacked the belief that they could ever achieve the goals that had been set for themselves.

As a way of getting them to focus on what they wanted to achieve, rather than what they have failed to achieve, I had them think of a time when they had accomplished something of great significance, a successful accomplishment at work. They were able to relive the emotion and more importantly remember the state they were in and what they did that made them a success.

Success breeds success.

If you have done it once, you have the potential to do it again.

A couple of weeks later, I had a phone call from the director to say the individual who had struggled the most had gone on to hit all of her targets three months in a row. WOW.

When she was asked what caused the dramatic change and difference, she said to the director that the programme gave her the confidence and ability to produce results and because her focus was now different, her vision for success now established in her mind, nothing seemed impossible.

SECRET NO.5

Praise *and* Encouragement

PRAISE AND ENCOURAGEMENT

Another practical tool to unlocking the potential of your team is embedded in "Praise and Encouragement".

When team members are acknowledged, encouraged and praised for what they have done, it is amazing to see the extra mile that they will be prepared to go for the business.

So, here is a very useful and practical tool that you can use straight away.

Schedule praise sessions to acknowledge success and progress. These will help to add value to the individual. When you give those praise sessions, be specific about what you are praising them for. Relate it to an actual accomplishment and how it added value to them, to the team and business.

A great exercise that is guaranteed to achieve a successful outcome is to bring everyone together every six to eight weeks over some nice food and drinks (don't overindulge) to share progress on how everyone's actions are contributing to the success of the business. The words that you use as a team are paramount to the level of motivation that is displayed within the team.

Words are powerful and create.

By your words, you can create the atmosphere that will

either motivate or demotivate your team.

Choose words as a team that should formulate the team daily vocabulary – this will help combat negativity and create a much more positive and fun environment. Words also energise and change the state of the individual.

The following words/phrases might help:

That's an awesome…

Your work is exemplary.

You are doing great.

That is excellent.

Your attitude at work is amazing.

Thank you for…

You are a real asset.

You are outrageously fun to work with.

I am happy to see…

I appreciate your support.

I love your energy.

In embracing this secret, you are not only helping the individual to feel part of the team and the business, but also collectively as a team, they are all striving towards the same objectives.

SECRET NO.6

Training
and Coaching

TRAINING AND COACHING

I would say that this is one of the most important secrets to motivating your teams. Getting them to achieve outstanding results and be at the top of their game requires "Training and Coaching".

I am often amazed at the lack of training that team members receive.

At the beginning of my training programmes, I often ask the participants to share with me the last time they upgraded their skills or had any personal development training. It is shocking to find out that some have gone as far as 10 years without any training or coaching input, and yet, businesses wonder why their teams are demotivated.

Research proves that money is often at the bottom of the list when it comes to motivating employees. Employees would rather you invested in them, developing their skills and talents, and adding value to who they are. They would prefer the investment rather than a massive pay cheque (although that helps as well).

Training and coaching is designed to improve individual performance. The more you train your team and give them opportunities to progress, the more you will both enjoy the benefits it brings.

As a business it is crucial to commit time, a healthy

budget and energy to developing your people.

It is a well-known fact that businesses who are passionate and committed to the personal development of their staff yield tremendous results.

Schedule regular team development days at least once every quarter with the help of an external coach or facilitator. Refuse the temptation to do it on the cheap, by doing it yourself or getting a team member to run the session. There is a real difference in the outcomes.

Development days should be taken seriously and respected as an opportunity to gain new knowledge, challenge yourself and others, and create a platform for sharing ideas and growing.

By doing it yourself or getting a fellow team member to do it, there may not be much learning or varied perspectives, as you may be tempted to play safe and not rock the boat with your team members. The idea is to learn together. The result - the team member might be reluctant to open up or even share ideas, because they see it as another team meeting rather than a team development day to update their knowledge and skills.

Harnessing the poor excuse of not having enough money or time to develop your staff means that you will be stuck with a demotivated and average workforce, because the best ones would have gone to organisations that are committed to developing them and helping them raise their standards.

The smart ones, who are hungry for success, will invest personally in their development and then apply somewhere else for promotion.

In the end as a business, you will be left with those who are not really bothered one way or the other – I call them 'Seat Warmers'. They will provide the bare minimum to get by until retirement hits them.

In the meantime, as a business, you are being overtaken by your competitors, and worst case scenario, you may have to close the business.

It means you had so much 'dead weight' in your boat that it sank.

Teams as a whole, need feedback on how they are functioning and producing results. They need someone who is external to give them perspective and guidance and help energise and motivate them.

SECRET NO.7

R.O.W.E

RESULT ONLY WORK ENVIRONMENT (ROWE)

An awesome secret to motivating your team is to consider a Result Only Work Environment (ROWE).

This is a great model and some forward thinking businesses are switching over and recognising this work model, which asks employees to provide a certain amount of work (results) rather than asking them to work for a certain amount of time, which is the old traditional way of doing things, using the traditional 8 to 4 or 9 to 5, five days a week model.

The ROWE principle is about creating a working environment that is geared towards recognising and rewarding outcomes and results rather than time.

The faster a team or a team member can complete a task or hit a target to the recognised standard, the sooner they can be rewarded.

This ultimately will be seen as a challenge and will in turn encourage the team to perform at a much higher level of motivation.

In implementing ROWE, it is important that you, as the manager or team leader, are clear about what you want to achieve on a daily, weekly or monthly basis. The clearer the objectives and framework, the more likely the team will be able to produce the required results.

You can give it a go by informing your team if they achieve a certain milestone, let us say by Friday lunchtime, all team members can have the afternoon off. You would be pleasantly surprised how super productive they can become.

Remember, in ROWE, reward is based on actual output, not hours, so productivity is likely to soar. Using this principle will help increase everyone's focus on quality.

SECRET NO.8

Saying
Thank You

SAYING THANK YOU

Another secret to motivating your team is embedded in the simple form of "Saying Thank You".

As simple as that may sound, it goes a long way towards getting your teams motivated. So, make a particular point of thanking them for anything above and beyond the call of duty. Let them know you noticed and that you are grateful.

Here is a winning practical strategy.

Make or buy a card for each team member. Thank them for something they have done for you. Make it personal. It could be their positive attitude, or the fact that they always remember to make you a drink or they take time to listen to you.

Post the cards for an extra added impact. Make a conscious effort to find something to thank them for regularly.

A few years ago, I gave a presentation at a business conference in London. One of the areas I spoke about was the value of saying thank you. In my usual style of getting the audience to participate, I got them to turn to the person next to them and to thank them for being their partner during the conference.

After the conference a young lady approached me with a beaming smile on her face, took hold of my hand and said: "I just wanted to say thank you for your presentation. I was sitting next to my boss during your thank you exercise and for the first time since I started working with the company, she thanked me for all the work that I have been doing. I feel appreciated now, so thank you for that exercise."

Saying thank you energises your staff to give their very best. It puts a smile on their face and makes them feel valued and appreciated. It is indeed your gateway to creating a productive team.

SECRET NO.9

Trust-*Based Environment*

TRUST-BASED ENVIRONMENT

A "Trust-Based Environment" is another secret to motivating your team.

Without trust, your team cannot be effective. Without trust, your team is unlikely to share information or ideas and skills. It means your team members are working individually rather than collectively. So, building a trust-based environment is critical to the success of a great and effective team.

A trust-based environment can be built by having team development days. This is where team members get to know and appreciate each other, and subsequently get to be more open.

When that environment is built, you can guarantee that your team will soar. And when they soar, they will produce great and outstanding results.

SECRET NO.10

Let **Go**

LET GO

My final secret to motivating your team is to "Let go".

Let go of some control.

Micromanagement is a motivation killer and you do not have to control each and every task they do. Allow them to inject and appreciate their uniqueness. Stop telling them how to do their job – instead set expectations of results.

I once coached a businesswoman who had a real issue in letting go. She wanted to control everything around her. This created a lot of tension in the office as her staff were frightened and lacked the confidence in making any decisions without her consent.

The result was such that no one took responsibility. They produced the bare minimum that they could get away with. In the end she became more and more stressed as she had to do most of the work herself.

Letting go of some control is the solution to empowering your team. It gives them the space to grow and gain confidence in their ability and skills. They are able to take responsibility for their mistakes and learn without fear or anxiety. They can exercise their decision-making muscles.

On the other hand, you can be assured that they will produce the desired results for the business even in your absence.

Delegation is therefore the key to the success of a high performing team.

Here are some easy to implement actions to get you started.

Give individuals more responsibility for their own job and action.

Convey your expectations, but allow them to choose the best way to produce the outcome.

Let them learn from their mistakes. Encourage them to use their intelligence, skills and talent rather than expect them to always do it your way or act like robots.

Be strong and confident enough to accept that you cannot always control everything.

Delegation has great benefits, not only for you, as in freeing up more time, but also for your team. By delegating, you are able to test out the ability and potential of your team. Refuse the temptation to delegate the jobs that you hate or dislike.

Conclusion

CONCLUSION

So, the secret to motivating your teams is to make them feel they are participating in something valuable, unique and out of the ordinary. It is about committing to a higher cause that is greater than theirs. The commitment becomes priceless.

Now, business sceptics may say - "what if we train and invest in our people and they leave?"

Well think about this - "What if you do not train and invest in them and they stay?"

So, by applying these ten secrets, you truly have the power to motivate and transform both individual and business performance thereby taking your team to the highest level of success.

As the director of a coaching and training business, this realisation has helped in my own recruitment strategies, making sure that individual visions and values are in alignment to the overall business vision and that they are fully communicated. I have also created coaching tools and strategies in combating negativity in teams and instilling a positive mind-set for building outstanding teams that are energised, take ownership, share ideas more openly and function cooperatively and creatively.

What are you waiting for?

Our Team Transformation programmes are designed to help you implement and embed these secrets by getting your team to be a high performing team, bursting with energy, focused and operating in clarity. This will enable them to make great decisions that will bring and yield dividend for your business.

ABOUT JOY OGEH-HUTFIELD

Joy Ogeh-Hutfield

Trained by the renowned international coach Anthony Robbins, Joy Ogeh-Hutfield has been working as a leadership and team transformation coach with various organisations and businesses for a number of years.

Joy came to realise that having demotivated teams is the number one reason why businesses are often losing money. When teams lack confidence, clarity and seldom understand why they do what they do, they are unable to perform at their best to meet their targets, let alone unleash their full potential to produce outstanding results.

She is the founder of Joy Transformation, a dynamic and innovative coaching business that will work with you and your business to maximise results by creating a winning mind-set.

Her coaching style is a massive, positive call to action that has already powerfully impacted many individuals and organisations.

TAKE ACTION

If you want to take advantage of the unique opportunity to build a 'Transformational Team' that will generate soaring sales, increased productivity, renewed energy and commitment, and greater team morale and retention, contact Joy Ogeh-Hutfield today at:

JOY TRANSFORMATION COACHING

www.joytransformationcoach.com

Telephone: +44 (0) 1792 535272

Email: info@joytransformationcoach.com

"Joy brings high energy but balances it with an extremely motivational and inspiring approach to her work. She has a unique ability to bring out the best in individuals and teams, filling them with confidence, renewed focus and drive. Her impact is long lasting and powerful, and I have great pleasure in recommending Joy." **Michael Downie, General Manager at Marriott International.**

"Joy has a very unique method of stimulating thinking and delivering leadership content. The effect on certain individuals has been remarkable. There has been a renewed energy in our leadership and already we've seen some significant changes in behavior." **Ian Fowler, Director of Radio at UTV Media GB.**

Lightning Source UK Ltd.
Milton Keynes UK
UKOW06f2255121015